THE COSMIC CRIMINAL

The Case Against Grace

THE COSMIC CRIMINAL

The Case Against Grace

CAROLYN CHAMBERS

The Cosmic Criminal
Carolyn Chambers

Library of Congress Cataloging-in-Publication Data

The Cosmic Criminal – The Case Against Grace
Printed in the United States of America
ISBN: 978-0-9967582-6-0

Cover design by CW Technology Consulting

www.anointedlifepublishing.com

Table of Contents

Preface vii

Introduction ix

Chapter 1 Grace vs. Perception 1

Chapter 2 Grace vs. Unbelief 7

Chapter 3 Grace vs. Fear 17

Chapter 4 Grace vs. Care 25

Chapter 5 Grace vs. Doubt 33

Chapter 6 Grace vs. Pleasant Knowledge 39

Chapter 7 The Processes of Grace 43

Chapter 8 Possessing Your Possessions 81

Conclusion 89

Epilogue 93

The Grace Roadmap 95

Salvation Prayer 97

About the Author 99

Special Thanks

The kingdom of God is for seekers...special thanks to all seekers, both near and far.

And special thanks to my husband, Keith, whose contributions humanized the concepts and made them exceptionally clear.

And of course, much heart-felt thanks and appreciation to the Holy Spirit whose empowering powers are so amazing.

Preface
This book is about:

Two Kingdoms
Two Instructions
Two Battles &
One Victory

We are citizens of the kingdom of light. This kingdom is responsible for our total welfare and happiness. In executing its duties, the kingdom responds to our needs by way of grace. We receive this grace as a prompting. When a response of faith is received by God, then victory is always the outcome.

From time to time, grace is disrupted by another kingdom, which is the kingdom of darkness. Its promptings appeal to the sense realm; its outcome is dismay. This book was written to share the cause and effect of this conflict and its impact on us as kingdom citizens.

For our rejoicing is this, the testimony of our conscience...not with fleshly wisdom, but by the grace of God...

(2 Corinthians 1:12, KJV)

Introduction

The case of the cosmic criminal can be seen in an experience a woman had after she married a man with children. They were actually young adults. They loved their father, and they were happy to still have him in their lives. Along with the wife, all shared the good times. Whereas they appropriately called him 'dad,' it dawned on the wife that they were calling her by her first name.

Following tradition, the wife asked that they call her either mom, step-mom, or some form thereof; not by her first name. But, they unanimously refused.

The wife tried time after time to get them to follow her request, even asking the father to intervene and use his influence, but his children still refused to be persuaded.

The more she asked, the stronger they remained in their stand.

Eventually, this stance began to put a strain on the family relationship.

One day, while the kids were visiting their dad, the wife noticed that she was bombarded with a barrage of vexing thoughts. The difference was so noticeable that she asked herself: *Where are all these thoughts coming from, and what happened to my peace?*

She realized that the thoughts came during the visitation. Bewildered, she then asked herself: *What am I doing wrong? Why has my peace been taken?*

At that moment she was led to pick up the Bible. It landed on 1 Corinthians 9:22, where Paul used his freedom to become a servant unto all, that he might gain the more. Paul then explained how it worked: "...to the weak became I as weak that I might gain the weak..." At that moment, the wife knew where she had missed it.

Whereas love is adaptable, she had been insisting on her own rights and her own desires. Her convictions, although noble, violated kingdom law—the Law of Love. Her care disrupted the <u>flow of grace</u> and forced her to operate in the law of sin and death. She had given place to the enemy. Now he had legality over her and, he came after her peace of mind. She had been taken captive.

Although no law of the land had been violated, she had <u>breached</u> (broken) spiritual law, and that's exactly what the enemy watches for: a breach. Now, it was a case against grace:

Her case: Belief in her convictions. Her breach: Tradition made her a cosmic criminal. She failed to follow the love law.

We become cosmic criminals when we sin against the empowering power of grace, limiting God. Grace can be defined as the divine influence of God upon our hearts.

As it flows, we are then able to tap into God's limitless (cosmic) powers and we become unstoppable; that is, until God's grace is disrupted. Then, it becomes a case: *a legal process* that must be litigated by *scripture*. And, because cosmic crimes carry cosmic ramifications, they affect our divine destiny. That is, they inhibit our ability to access the grace needed to crucify fleshly wisdom. We are thus confined to the natural, sight realm—where we lean to our own understanding.

Needless to say, grace again flowed to the wife as she received her revelation, and her peace of mind returned.

The children still call by her first name, but she is no longer offended by it. And, they all continue to enjoy the good times.

In this book, you will find seven *fail-proof* processes that <u>keep us</u> in the grace of God. Each process shows a unique facet of God's grace that is available and how *certain influences* hinder its flow.

More importantly, you will see that when grace is received, destruction is averted. However, when it is not received, destruction is inevitable.

You will also find, throughout this book, <u>select scriptures</u> that I refer to as: God's Alerts. These 'Alerts' are scriptures that depict a directive from the Lord: an instruction telling us *what*, *why*, and *how* a particular virtue is to be performed. And, they are used to litigate each case.

- **What:** refers to the <u>wisdom</u> of the scripture.
- **Why:** gives us its <u>understanding</u>
  How: is the <u>knowledge</u>; it tells us how the scripture is to be applied.

Each alert ends with a <u>commentary</u> on the thoughts and intents of God's heart that can be seen when wisdom, understanding, and knowledge function as a whole.

That in the ages to come he might shew the exceeding riches of his grace in his kindness toward us through Christ Jesus.

(Ephesians 2:7)

Chapter 1

Grace vs. Perception

Grace, often described as God's underlined: unmerited kindness, was offered to a young man by the name of Hanun. His story is told in 2 Samuel 10. Hanun's father had recently passed away. When King David heard the news, he sent a few of his servants to Hanun to offer his condolences; seeking to comfort him.

After hearing the words of comfort, Hanun's men told him that David was not sincere; that he instead wanted to spy out the land and even overthrow it. Being tempted by his own desire, Hanun was naturally enticed to follow the perspective he had received from his men.

Now, it was a case against grace:

Hanun's case: He trusted his own perception. His breach: Perception made Hanun a cosmic criminal. Now this case must be litigated by scripture. He failed to acknowledge God; he was half-hearted.

Leaning to his own understanding, Hanun insulted David's men by shaving off one-half of their beards and cutting their robes—and thus exposing their buttocks. Knowing that a battle would ensue, Hanun then obtained help from a neighboring army. However, the help was insufficient, and they were all defeated. That war left over forty-seven thousand men slain.

By rejecting grace, Hanun could not access help from the spiritual realm. He was then forced to turn to the natural realm. But again, without grace, the natural realm was also powerless. So destruction came. Hanun's fall from grace was due solely to his perception: his own mental impression of the situation. And that *perception* caused thousands of lives to be devoured.

Breaches

In the fiftieth chapter of Jeremiah, the Bible gives us a behind the scenes look at the reaction of the enemy once we have fallen from grace: "All that found them have devoured them: and their adversaries said: we offend not, because they have sinned against the LORD…" (Jeremiah 50:7).

The enemy is, in effect, saying: "We are not guilty; they sinned, having destroyed themselves by falling from grace."

A fall from grace creates a breach. Each breach will cause us to miss God. When the children of Israel failed to take the promise land, God said they shall know His *breach* of promise. (See Num. 14:34)

Breaches *(infractions)* occur when we fail to be good stewards of the manifold grace of God.

3

Manifold refers to the multifaceted influences of grace on our lives—whether we are facing mountains, hills, or valleys. When grace is received, it becomes our sufficiency. This influence is sufficient against distresses, infirmities, weaknesses, and persecutions.

When the influence of grace enters our hearts, God is conducting King to king business with us as covenant, mature sons and daughters of the kingdom of God; perception, doubt, unbelief, fear, care, and even pleasant knowledge have no place in that kingdom.

Although grace is necessary for success and survival, it may be frustrated or taken in vain. But when it is found, signs and wonders take place. Noah, in building the Ark, found grace. Esther found grace with King Ahasuerus that enabled her to deliver her people from destruction. Even Ruth found grace with Boaz and was delivered out of poverty.

The Perception Alert

This alert calls for us to see things from a proper point of view: God's perception. It keeps us from being <u>half-hearted</u>, and our hearts from being divided. (See Hosea 10:2)

What: "Trust in the LORD with <u>all</u> thine heart;
Why: and lean not unto thine own understanding.
How: In <u>all</u> thy ways acknowledge Him, and He shall direct thy paths"

(Proverbs 3:5-6).

To prevent our hearts from being divided, we need to acknowledge Him—our Helper. The half-hearted have hearts that are divided; subsequently, they are found faulty. They are not fully persuaded and they act prematurely.

That being justified by his grace, we should be made heirs according to the hope of eternal life.

(Titus 3:7)

Chapter 2

Grace vs. Unbelief

In John, Chapter 5, the story is told of the man at the pool of Bethesda, waiting for his healing. The Bible says he had an infirmity for thirty-eight years. Aware of his situation, Jesus asked the man would he be made whole; He wanted to know the man's perception of his situation. In other words, what were the <u>legal grounds</u> that the enemy was using against him?

The man was happy to comply; he wanted to plead his case. He contended, "Sir, I have no man, when the water is troubled, to put me into the pool: but while I am coming, another steppeth down before me" (John 5:7).

Jesus saw that the man had faith, for he kept coming to the pool. Nevertheless, he was having difficulty accessing grace. And the Bible said Jesus knew that he had been in that <u>case</u>, a long time. The man's thought: *I have no man to put me into the pool...I need help*, was never challenged, so it was never resisted. He therefore remained in that state for thirty-eight years; justified by the flesh. This caused him to miss the mark. Now, it was a case against grace:

His case: He justified his condition. His breach: Unbelief made this man a cosmic criminal. Now this case must be litigated by scripture. He failed to take captive his thoughts of unbelief.

Unbelief is the sin from which all other sins come. It is received by believing something God did not say; it always begins with a lie, and it ends with a scenario designed to entice us to believe a lie. It works by enticing us to second-guess our beliefs. It actually puts us at odds with our own conscience; then we become faithless and sin against grace.

After hearing his case, Jesus began by giving the man an instruction which was <u>contrary</u> to his own thoughts. He had to attack the man's unbelief. He said, 'Rise, take up thy bed, and walk.'

Rise—take captive your thoughts.

Take up your bed— take control.

Walk—tread down the wicked (flesh)

When the man obeyed, he was immediately made whole. He then realized that he did not need help, he needed grace.

In Philippians 4, Paul declares that we *can* do all things through Christ who strengthens us. So when we say: "*I can't,*" it then becomes a sin against grace.

As this man resisted his carnal thoughts, he was able to go free. That same freedom was available to him 38 years earlier, if he had not been hindered by unbelief.

A Man at Odds with Himself

When we yield to the carnal nature, we are, in fact, at odds with our own conscience. Luke 15 calls such a person, the 'lost son.'

In this story, the younger son, under the influence of his flesh, asked for his inheritance from his father. He had decided to go it alone. Not realizing it, he was also leaving the realm of faith and would not be able to access God's grace. This alone would make him a cosmic criminal.

True to form, he wasted all his substance on riotous living. Disillusioned, he then made the only decision that he could—he decided to confront himself. According to the Bible, he came to *himself* and said, "I will arise and go [walk] to my father."

Arise: —take captive my thoughts.
Walk: —tread down the wicked (flesh).

The Bible said: "He arose and came to his father." In pleading his case, he told his father that he had sinned against heaven (this made the crime cosmic) and against him.

This story illustrates that our sin nature backs down as soon as it is confronted with wisdom contrary to itself. Judgment is then rendered to the flesh, and it is crucified. With the flesh crucified, the father gladly received his son back.

Protecting the Grace

Although grace is, by far, the most powerful force in the universe; incapable of being conquered, invincible, and embodying fearlessness, it must still be protected and honored, as if it were the quarterback on your team. However, as you have seen, its flow can be unduly hindered or stopped by competing and contaminating influences of unbelief.

These influences attempt to move us from God's grace into another gospel. Confused, we will often try to second-guess ourselves, believing that we have a choice. However, in reality, when that happens, a contaminating intercept has actually already taken place; by our sin nature: *the flesh.*

The challenge is, when we have heard the divine influence of grace; it must be heeded; for it is the voice of our conscience speaking. Needless to say, our conscience cannot be answered, only obeyed. If there is an answer, it comes from the flesh, and both the conscience and the flesh can't occupy the same space at the same time. So, as soon as the conscience is answered, (intercepted) you have lost. You are then a man at odds with himself: his own conscience. Afterwards, when things go amiss, you will find yourself saying, "I should have followed my first mind."

I Almost Missed It

I received the prompting to give a new book away. But, before obeying this prompting, I thought about it to see if I would perhaps need it later. Realizing what I was doing, I caught myself. I smiled, and the Holy Spirt said: "You had to first check with your flesh." I quickly mailed the book and the person was very blessed.

The Wicked Responds to Grace

The Bible says that there are times when God had to use the voice of others to speak the influence of grace into our hearts. The Bible shows that Pharaoh (a type of flesh) was one such example. God sent Moses to tell him to let his people go. Pharaoh questioned this wisdom, saying, "Who is the Lord that I should obey his voice to let Israel go? I know not the Lord, neither will I let Israel go" (Exodus 5:2).

This shows that the flesh truly does not know God, and is not <u>trying</u> to know God. His goal is to run interference as soon as Godly wisdom is sown into our hearts; especially words of grace. This interference often begins with a question and, of course, ends with unbelief. Consequently, Pharaoh and his army were all eventually drowned. Obeying that God-sent voice would have, at the least, saved their lives.

Grace is protected when we contend; literally fight for the faith that was *once* delivered into our hearts. (See Jude) Through faith, we fight unbelief; then grace is accessed and limits are taken off of God.

The Unbelief Alert

This alert prepares us to resist unbelief as we stand fast; holding fast to our faith, confidence, and profession (confession).

What: "Take heed, brethren,
Why: lest there be in any of you an evil heart of unbelief, in departing from the living God.

What: But exhort one another daily…
Why: lest any of you be hardened through the deceitfulness of sin.
How: For we are made partakers of Christ, if we hold the beginning of our confidence stedfast unto the end" (Hebrews 3:12-14).

Take heed, the sin of unbelief is defeated as we endure to the end.

I marvel that ye are so soon removed from him that called you into the grace of Christ unto another gospel.

(Galatians 1:6)

Chapter 3

Grace vs. Fear

The prophet Elijah found himself in a similar predicament (helplessness) as the man at the pool of Bethesda. I call it the Pool of Bethesda Syndrome. In this case, Elijah perceived that he was the only one left serving God—the only righteous one. And after being threatened, he was on the run for his life. This threat attacked his imagination. Now, it was a case against grace:

Elijah's case: He felt threatened.

His breach: Fear made Elijah a cosmic criminal. Now this case must be litigated by scripture. He failed to stand his ground.

Feeling threatened, Elijah found himself a cave and decided to lodge there. God asked him what he was doing there, and Elijah began to plead his case:

"I have been very jealous for the LORD God of hosts: because the children of Israel have forsaken thy covenant, thrown down thine altars, and slain thy prophets with the sword; and I, even I only, am left; and they seek my life, to take it away" (1 Kings 19:10).

Elijah's behavior is perplexing. He was able to access the grace necessary to destroy <u>450</u> false prophets of Baal, but he became fearful in accessing that same grace to defeat <u>one</u>: Jezebel, the wife of the wicked king of Israel, who had threaten to take his life.

In the natural, we would say, *yea, you win some and lose some.* Or, *you can't win them all.* That is also what the Syrians said when they were fighting with the children of Israel. They told their king that the Lord is the God of the hills, but He is not God of the valleys. However, God begged to differ and proved that He is the God of all. (See 1 Kings 20:23; 28)

So, God redeemed Elijah: He called him by name. Then, He edified Elijah and gave him an instruction that was contrary to his own thoughts. He had to get him to resist fear. God said: "Go forth, and <u>stand</u> upon the mount." In other words, stand your ground. Take control. As Elijah took his <u>stand</u>, various temptations threatened his peace, but this time he was not moved. He had learned that he had to fight, to stand.

So Elijah waited for the *'still small'* voice of God. After hearing it, he went out and <u>stood</u> at the entrance of the cave; for he would no longer lodge there—he had changed his mind. God asked him again, saying, "What are you doing here?"

Elijah repeated his story, but now, he was no longer a man at odds with himself. He had become fearless.

And having received empowering grace, he *stood* in his authority.

God then gave Elijah three assignments and some *inside* information. He said: "Yet I have left me seven thousand in Israel, all the knees which have not bowed unto Baal, and every mouth which hath not kissed him" (1 Kings 19:18).

And God proved it. Elijah was able to *see* that his successor, Elisha, was one of those who had not bowed the knee to Baal. Elijah found Elisha in the field plowing with twelve yokes of oxen and he with the twelfth.

Elisha knew how to handle the flesh. By not bowing the knee, he did twice as many miracles as Elijah did—for he received a double portion of Elijah's anointing.

Faint, Yet Pursuing

Gideon, on the other hand, took his stand in grace <u>despite</u> his fear.

In Judges 6, the Israelites were severely oppressed, and they were greatly impoverished after being invaded by the Midianites: And so it was, when Israel had sown, the Midianites came up, and the Amalekites, and the children of the east, even they came up against them. They destroyed the increase of the earth, and left no sustenance for Israel: neither sheep, nor ox, nor ass. God then called Gideon to deliver Israel.

At that time, Gideon was threshing wheat by the winepress, as to hide *it* from the Midianites. While he hid, the angel of the Lord appeared unto him and called him by his redemptive name saying, "The Lord is with thee, thou mighty man of valor."

Why was God with Gideon, and why was he called a mighty man of valor?

It was because he had responded to the influence of grace on his heart. He had received a contrary instruction (*thresh wheat by the winepress*) and he obeyed it. His obedience made him a mighty man. To obey grace, Gideon had to fight his own fleshly wisdom. When he did, he passed God's test. He had been faithful in little; God could trust him to be faithful in much.

Gideon's readiness to respond to grace allowed God's will to be done in the earth. He could now intervene on behalf of the Israelites. God said: "Go in thy might and thou shall save Israel from the Midianites." However, conquering the Midianites was not an easy task. And it took some time.

The Bible said that Gideon was faint, yet pursuing. In other words, he never allowed his fear to stop him from responding to the influence of grace on his heart. As a result, the enemy was subdued and the country was in quiet for forty years.

The Fear Alert

This alert declares that we are redeemed
by the name we call it: call it healed, count
it all joy; call your lack a full supply.

What: "...Fear not:
Why: for I have redeemed thee,
How: I have called thee by thy name; thou
art mine" (Isaiah 43:1).

When you call it by its redemptive
name, you have nothing to fear.

And God *is* able to make all grace abound toward you; that ye, always having all sufficiency in all *things*, may abound to every good work.

(2 Corinthians 9:8)

Chapter 4

Grace vs. Care

The Bible is replete with stories of people pleading their case against grace. Consider the case of Martha. According to Luke 10:38-42, a certain woman named Martha received Jesus into her house. And she had a sister called Mary, who <u>also</u> sat at Jesus' feet and heard His word.

However, Martha was distressed. Pleading her case, she said, "Lord, dost thou not <u>care</u> that my sister has left me to serve alone?"

Now, it was a case against grace: *Martha's case: Legitimate care. Her breach: Care made Martha a cosmic criminal.*

Now this case must be litigated by scripture. She failed to cast her care.

Care had reduced Martha to a state of immaturity. Left in that state, she would have surely been unable to possess her possessions; thereby robbing her of her inheritance. Her care had to be confronted.

Jesus answered and said unto her, "Martha, Martha, thou art careful and troubled about many things: But one thing is needful: and Mary hath chosen that good part, which shall not be taken away from her."

Jesus edified Martha by addressing both the cause and the effect of her issue:

Cause: Care
Effect: Being Troubled

Martha said she needed help. Jesus disagreed. Help is not the problem. Jesus said the real issue is that you are full of <u>care</u>, and your care is <u>troubling</u> you.

Seed Sown into Good Ground

Jesus had spoken to both Martha and Mary; the Bible said Mary <u>also</u> sat at Jesus' feet.

However, when the seeds were sown, they never reached Martha's heart. They were intercepted by the <u>cares</u> of this world that troubled her and choked the seed. That made her unfruitful.

Mary, on the other hand, knew the value of protecting her heart—she did not allow cares to intercept and take the seed Jesus had sown. Her ground was then able to produce up to a 100 fold return.

After Jesus edified Martha, she changed, for in John 12:2, the Bible says there was a supper made for Jesus, and Martha served. Her heart was now free of care, for she had cast it all.

When we yield to care, we place ourselves in a position of being devoured by the adversary. Care creates a breach and we become cosmic criminals. As you already know, the cosmic criminal commits a crime against the kingdom of God. According to one pastor, "The police may not see you run that red light, but the devil did." And he is looking for breaches.

For most Christians, the devil may have great difficulty enticing us to rob a bank. But when it comes to crimes against the kingdom (cosmic), he may have a better shot. This is what Daniel's enemies thought when they tried to set him up to fall from grace.

According to the book of Daniel, chapter 6:4-5: "The presidents and princes sought to find occasion against Daniel concerning the kingdom; but they could find none occasion nor fault; forasmuch as he was faithful, neither was there any error or fault found in him."

The Bible goes on to say: "Then said these men, we shall not find any occasion against this Daniel, except we find it against him concerning the law of his God."

So they plotted to get Daniel to violate the influence of grace on his heart. They wanted him to stop his daily prayers. And if he disobeyed, he would be thrown into a den of lions. That threat was even *reluctantly* backed up by the king, who admired Daniel. Daniel had a choice: should he obey God and continue to crucify his flesh by praying three times a day, or yield to the threat? He chose to continue in grace.

Daniel had an audience of One: God. His heart was not divided, and that allowed him to remain faithful. He simply stayed the course. Although Daniel was thrown into the lion's den, his heart was free of care. And without care, the lions could not devour him. There was no breach of covenant.

Standing against Care

The Bible shows how a man like Daniel was able to sustain such an attack against his faith. In the New Testament, it is seen as the 'flood attack.' (See Luke 6:48)

In this type of attack, the cares, concerns, doubts, fears, and unbelief all beat vehemently upon our souls and minds—but is unable to shake us—when we have cast our care. Because there was no *inner storm*, Daniel could withstand the outer storm.

We stand, proving our position of power. It says that our heart is established; that we are settled: not moved by evil tidings; just trusting God. (See Psalms 112)

The Power of Standing

- When Gideon and his men <u>stood</u>, all the host (enemy) ran, cried, and fled. (See Judges 6)
- When the king saw Esther <u>standing</u>, she obtained favor. (See Ester 5)
- As Ezra caused the people to understand the law, all the people <u>stood</u> in their place. (See Neh. 8:7)

These all withstood the storm as they stood in their place of authority.

The Care Alert

This alert declares that it is care that keeps the attack there!

What: "…be clothed with humility:
Why: for God resisteth the proud, and giveth grace to the humble.
What: Humble yourselves therefore under the mighty hand of God,
Why: that he may exalt you in due time:

What: Casting all your <u>care</u> upon him;
Why: for he careth for you.
How: Be sober, be vigilant; because your adversary the devil, as a roaring lion, walketh about, seeking whom he may devour: Whom resist stedfast in the faith…" (1 Peter 5:5-9).

The proud—those with care—are being resisted by God and devoured by the adversary.

And he said unto me, My grace is
sufficient for thee: for my strength
is made perfect in weakness.

Most gladly therefore will I rather
glory in my infirmities, that the
power of Christ may rest upon me.

Therefore I take pleasure in
infirmities, in reproaches, in
necessities, in persecutions, in
distresses for Christ's sake: for when
I am weak, then am I strong.

(2 Corinthians 12:9-10)

Chapter 5

Grace vs. Doubt

As kingdom citizens we have rights and privileges. In Luke 13, when Jesus noticed the woman who had been bound for eighteen years, He said that as a daughter of Abraham, she had a right to be loosed from her bonds.

When we know who we are in Christ and our rights as citizens, the only way we can become susceptible to <u>deception</u> is through doubt.

Doubt is the enemy's first line of attack. When doubt enters it does not come alone. It comes with loads of questions, innuendos, and also suspicions. We find ourselves undetermined, fearful, questioning our faith, unsettled, uncertain, focused on the difficulty, distrustful, and not decided; wavering, or staggering at the promises of God, and being slow or hesitant to believe.

Although grace is available, we are unable to partake of the deliverance it offers, being bound by doubt. Limits are then placed on God and the work of faith ceases. We are then deemed unstable and double-minded.

Doubt often occurs in areas where our capabilities are untested. Here, we tend to yield to the natural perspective, and we then lean to our own understanding. This response; however, carries a twofold penalty: We sin against grace and also fail to possess our possessions.

The Sky is the Limit

On one occasion, the Holy Spirit was prompting me to write my own 501c3, which is an IRS tax-exempt designation for charitable, non-profit organizations.

I had no previous experience in this area so naturally I reasoned that I needed some help. Now, it was a case against grace: *My case: Seeing the difficulty. My breach: Doubt made me a cosmic criminal. Now this case must be litigated by scripture. I failed to resist doubt by faith.*

Although doubt controlled my perspective, my frame of reference; the Holy Spirit would not leave me alone. Every morning He was there urging me to complete the form. So finally, I sought outside help. I will never forget what this lawyer told me.

First, he said that he would charge me. I'm like, "Ok."

He then said, "But if I write it, you will still have to give me all the information that goes on the form." That was the turning point for me. I thought, *If that's the case, I can do it myself. Why would I pay him and supply him with all the information?*

That thought was an eye opener. It made me confront myself. As I changed my mind I was instantly connected to my faith. Then I felt empowered to follow the divine influence of God upon my heart.

So, I eagerly picked up the packet of information and reviewed it, again. And wow! I "gracefully," understood everything. I became so good that I found myself even reading the fine print—I had become an expert. I knew that after the packet of information was turned in, it would pass all the criteria. I had no doubt. For weeks that which I thought I couldn't do, was a 'piece of cake,' when grace entered the picture.

After the form was completed and I took it to the post office to mail it, the Holy Spirit said to me: "The sky is the limit." Needless to say, the form was approved, immediately. I had tapped into God's empowering grace. All that I needed to do was to keep the doubt out. These days you will find me saying the words: 'I can do it!'

The Doubt Alert

This alert shows how doubt exchanges our faith in God for faith in self. When doubt enters, it causes the work of faith to cease.

What: "…Have faith in God.
Why: For verily I say unto you,
How: That whosoever shall say unto this mountain, Be thou removed, and be thou cast into the sea; and shall <u>not doubt</u> in his heart, but shall believe that those things which he saith shall come to pass; he shall have whatsoever he saith" (Mark 11:22-23).

Doubt is the enemy's most subtle weapon. It includes: asking questions, being hesitant, being undetermined, being slow to believe, horror, fear, dread, apprehension, suspicion; withholding confidence, distrust, withholding assent, wavering, and seeing the difficulty. *It is resisted by faith.*

Let us therefore come boldly unto the throne of grace that we may obtain mercy, and find grace to help in time of need.

(Hebrews 4:16)

Chapter 6

Grace vs. Pleasant Knowledge

In 2 Samuel 13, the story is told of Amnon, a son of King David, who loved his step-sister, Tamar. The Bible said he was so vexed—being sick for her. And, because she was a virgin, that made things even more difficult for him.

However, he had a friend, whom the Bible described as subtil (cunning), and he proceeded to give Amnon a plan whereby he could manipulate his father into sending Tamar to him. The deception worked. Now, it was a case against grace:

Amnon's case: Sense of entitlement. His breach: Pleasant knowledge made Amnon a cosmic criminal. Now this case must be litigated by scripture. He lacked discretion.

When Tamar arrived, he asked her to lie with him. But she refused saying, "Nay." She then explained the consequences to him, including the shame she would have to endure and the tarnishing of his character. Tamar specifically gave him a way out: "…speak to the king; he will not withhold me from you." In other words, we can do this the right way. But Amnon would not listen to wisdom. His fleshly knowledge was more pleasant to him. Being controlled by his own emotions, he forced her and lay with her. As she ran out the door crying, her brother, Absalom, perceived what had happened and eventually killed Amnon.

Tamar's words were sound, yet unpleasant to Amnon. Here again, because grace was refused, destruction flowed.

Because the *flesh attack* is typically against the unpleasant task, one pastor said, "When you have the choice of doing the pleasant task versus the unpleasant task, choose the task that is unpleasant."

The Pleasant Knowledge Alert

This alert sees pleasant knowledge as anything that justifies the flesh, yet is contrary to our divine destiny.

What: "When wisdom entereth into thine heart, and
Why: knowledge is pleasant unto thy soul;
How: Discretion shall preserve thee, understanding shall keep thee"
(Proverbs 2:10-11).

When knowledge is pleasant to the soul, discretion chooses wisdom.

As every man hath received the gift, even so minister the same one to another, as good stewards of the manifold grace of God.

(1 Peter 4:10)

Chapter 7

The Processes of Grace

In 1 Kings 18:41-44, as the prophet Elijah was praying for rain, he garnered the influence of grace that enabled him to continue watching and praying until he saw some sign of his confession: The rain is coming.

Elijah sent his servant to look for any sign of rain, and time after time, his servant returned saying, "...there is nothing." The servant said, in effect, I see no sign that your prayer is being answered. I see no sign of your confession of faith. But Elijah did not despair, he just said, "Go again." And after the seventh time, his servant saw a little cloud, the size of a man's hand. The servant finally saw what Elijah had been confessing.

The secret to Elijah's success can be seen in analyzing the particular path of grace he followed. Elijah tapped into that component of grace that empowered him to <u>endure till the end</u>. In the New Testament, this grace is known as *importunity*. You trouble the flesh. (Luke 11:8)

Convicted by our own Convictions

When grace is received, it gives us access to think on God's level. The case against grace focuses on areas where we fall from grace, frustrate the grace of God, or take the grace of God in vain. In any event, we are thinking on a lower level. And, as a result, we become cosmic criminals; being convicted by our <u>own</u> convictions. Our identity in Christ is also compromised.

We are then turned to immaturity, being separated from the grace needed to receive our inheritance.

But, that was not the case for the Apostle Paul. He valued grace: its processes and its components. In fact, grace was his <u>claim to fame</u>. He boldly said in 1 Corinthians 15:10, "I am what I am…by the grace of God…yet not I, but the grace of God which was with me."

We are aware that Paul wrote over two-thirds of the New Testament, and he gives all the credit to grace. It can then be surmised that if we want to fulfill the call of God on our lives, then we too must garner the powerful influence of grace, whether we are free or bound.

Grace in Captivity

In 2 Kings 5, the story is told of a servant girl who was taken captive out of the land of Israel. Her captor was a leper. Following the influence of grace: "…she said unto her mistress, Would God my lord were with the prophet that is in Samaria! For he would recover him of his leprosy.

And one went in, and told his lord, saying, thus and thus said the maid that is of the land of Israel."

Her lord, Naaman, willingly heeded her advice and was recovered of his leprosy. He then vowed to no longer serve other gods. By allowing grace to reign in her heart, her lord's heart was turned to the true God.

The servant girl's secret: The New Testament calls this component of grace: *No little kindness*. (See Acts 28:2)

Being held a captive, this little maid could have blamed Naaman and given him what he deserved: her contempt and anger. Instead, she saw his need—the condition of his heart, and she responded with grace. She gave him no little kindness. By binding her own flesh, she was free to serve grace.

In the following pages, I have outlined seven processes of grace that empower us to yield to the divine influences of the grace of God; they will prepare us to fight back.

1. Grace to Discern

Calling and Naming

This process of grace guards our *will*. It focuses on discerning: calling and naming. It involves the test of agreement where we align our will with God's will. *When you guard the will, provisions are also guarded.*

In the book of Genesis, God told Abram that he would be a father of multitudes. But Abram was 75 years old, and he was childless. Later, God then changed his name from Abram to Abraham. This redemptive name allowed Abraham to tap into his spiritual inheritance, where all was possible; he became righteousness conscious.

So, Abraham began calling those things that be not as though they were: He called himself a father of multitudes while he was still childless. By doing so, he denied *childlessness* the right to exist in his life.

Nevertheless, that process was not easy; Abraham and his wife, Sarah, failed to discern that *long patience* was required. That <u>err</u> interrupted the flow of grace, and caused them set-back after set-back—test after test.

But, when the final test came, Abraham was well prepared. At that time, he was called to sacrifice his only son, Isaac, as a burnt offering. Being in the dark, Isaac innocently asked him, "... but where *is* the lamb for a burnt offering?" Abraham accurately discerned the will of God and answered, "God will provide Himself a lamb for the burnt offering." And God did just that. Discerning the will of God allowed God's <u>provision to flow</u>.

Without us discerning <u>truth</u> from <u>falsehood</u>, our provisions and the flow of grace are blocked so that we too experience set-back after set-back. When that happens, leaning to our own understanding becomes the norm and ironically, our comfort.

Adam's Test

Adam found the grace to accurately discern: *call and name* every living creature. He was batting a thousand with God. However, when given the task of finding a help-meet, Adam realized that he did not see (*discern*) the creature that matched the name he was discerning in his heart: Eve. God was pleased. Adam had passed the test—as Eve was not yet on the earth. Now there was a heaven and earth agreement. This agreement was crucial, for it signaled that Adam's will had aligned with God's will. This delighted God, and He then made the woman. And, Adam was blessed.

I understand the testing process well. My mother used it to discern our hearts and to see if our wills differed from hers. She would call one of us and ask for a favor; for example: "Carolyn, come rub my feet." Then she would watch for my response. When my will matched hers, I had passed her test.

The Calling and Naming Alert

The Principle: This grace empowers us to say what we are discerning in our hearts, as we discern truth from falsehood.

What: "And out of the ground the LORD God formed every beast of the field, and every fowl of the air; and brought them unto Adam
Why: to see [discern] what he would <u>call</u> them:
How: and whatsoever Adam <u>called</u> every living creature, that was the <u>name</u> thereof. And Adam gave names to all cattle, and to the fowl of the air, and to every beast of the field; but for Adam there was not found an help meet for him" (Genesis 2:19-20).

Commentary: We must duly discern all imposters before our help can be revealed.

Failure to Discern

In 2 Kings 13:18-19, Elisha was visited by King Joash while he was on his death bed. "And he said to the king, take the arrows. And he took them. And he said unto the king of Israel, Smite upon the ground. And he smote thrice, and stayed. And the man of God was wroth with him, and said, Thou shouldest have smitten five or six times; then had thou smitten Syria till thou had consumed it: whereas now thou shalt smite Syria but thrice."

King Joash failed to discern the will of God. This failure limited God and God's provisions.

King Joash began in the spirit, but was bewitched into yielding to his flesh. After hitting the earth three times, he stopped—yielding to another thought: his own fleshly wisdom. He failed to discern the voice of the imposter (the flesh) from the voice of grace. That breach cost him the grace to consume the enemy.

It Can Be Done

In the book of Joshua, chapter 8, Joshua was fighting a city named Ai. In fighting that battle, Joshua walked in agreement with the influence of grace that was in his heart. He had no problem discerning the will of God. The Bible says twelve thousand fell that day, because Joshua refused to withdraw his hand once he stretched out his spear; until he had utterly destroyed all the inhabitants of Ai.

Numbers 33:55-56, explains why Joshua was so committed. The Lord said to the Israelites: "...if ye will not drive out the inhabitants of the land from before you; then it shall come to pass, that those which ye let remain of them shall be pricks in your eyes, and thorns in your sides, and shall vex you in the land wherein ye dwell."

"Moreover it shall come to pass, that I shall do unto you, as I thought to do unto them."

Joshua let <u>God</u> be his dread.

2. Grace to Overcome

Buying and Selling

This process of grace guards our *joy*. It focuses on overcoming: buying the truth and not selling it. It involves *buying (redeeming) the field,* (things that are contrary to us) to bring the soul in <u>alignment</u> with the spirit. *To guard joy is to guard the victory.*

For approximately a year I had been meditating on Psalms 45:1. It says: "My heart is inditing a good matter..." This verse is a powerful way to keep in touch with our spiritual disposition. Mary, the mother of Jesus, aligned her soul to her spiritual state of mind, as well. In Luke1:46-47, she said, "My soul doth magnify the Lord, and [because] my spirit hath rejoiced in God my Savior." She reasoned that if her spirit is rejoicing, she should rejoice as well; in as much as, a house divided cannot stand. So, she made sure that her mood matched the joy that was in her spirit.

Buying the Field

A few months ago, I had a dream where my spirit was taking control. It was intervening and effectively man-handling two unbelief spirits—and it was proclaiming a good report. That morning, during my devotion, I found myself battling doubt, fear, lies, confusion, and unbelief.

At which point, the Holy Spirit spoke to my heart and reminded me of the dream. Then, in my mind's eye, I could see the image of my spirit taking control, giving strict orders and the two unbelief spirits immediately submitting. The choice was clear: buy the lies that had stolen my joy, or the truth that I had seen in the dream. I bought the truth. It lined up with the Word: "My heart is inditing a good matter." I sold it all: doubt, fear, and unbelief. And, my joy returned. I was of good cheer.

With joy, I had bought the field, the ground were battles are fought. And, my turnaround was immediate.

The Buying and Selling Alert

The Principle: This grace empowers us to overcome as we surrender our own thoughts and beliefs in exchange for God's. It is a change of perspective. (See Matthew 16)

What: "Buy the truth,
Why: and sell it not;
How: also wisdom, and instruction, and understanding" (Proverbs 23:23).

Commentary: Those who buy wisdom understand that it often comes in the form of an instruction—one that is opposed to our fleshly wisdom. And, they refuse to sell (surrender) it.

To buy the truth is to buy the field. The field (things that are contrary to us), is the ground where battles are fought. The field is redeemed by counting it all joy. Joy is an antidote; it buys the field, liberates it, and gives us an immediate turnaround.

Failure to Buy

The Bible describes the kingdom as a treasure hidden in a field, which when a man finds, he hides, and for joy, sells all, and buys that field. (See Matthew 13:44)

However, in Mathew 25, Jesus said there were 10 virgins: five were wise and five were foolish. All were waiting for the bridegroom. The wise, following the influence of grace, bought extra oil. But the foolish did not. As the bridegroom was coming, the foolish noticed that their lamps were gone out; they had ignored the *instruction to* buy extra oil. They *thought* that what they had was enough. And, after their lamps were gone out, they *thought* that they could borrow from the wise. But, they were grievously mistaken.

As they held on to their own beliefs, and thoughts, the door was shut. Know that the foolish were given the same influence of grace as the wise, but failed *to buy it*; they chose to hold on to their own perspective.

3. Grace to Occupy

Hearing and Doing

This process of grace guards the *Word*. It focuses on the concept of occupying: being hearers and not doers only. It involves (occupying) seizing the Word that was sown in our hearts; *if you do not occupy you will lose what you thought you had.*

In the book of Jeremiah, chapter 35, Jeremiah was told to go to the house of the Rechabites and to bring them into the house of the Lord; then give them wine to drink. And, that is what Jeremiah did.

He set before them pots full of wine and cups and told them to drink the wine. However, they steadfastly refused, and they said that Jonadab, their father, commanded them not to drink wine, neither their sons, forever. They proceeded to say, "We are not to build houses nor sow neither seed nor plant vineyards nor have any. But we were told to just live in tents so that we may live many days in the land where we be strangers." They added, "We have obeyed the voice of our father in all that he has charged us, to drink no wine all our days, we, our wives, sons, nor daughters… we have obeyed and done according to all that Jonadab, our father, commanded us."

God commended the Rechabites, saying for until this day they do not drink, but obey their father's commandment and all his precepts. God said: "Tell them that their father, Jonadab shall not lack a man to <u>stand</u> before Me forever."

The Rechabites occupied the word that had been sown in their hearts. In the New Testament, this component of grace specifies: That unto every one which has shall be given. (See Luke 19:26)

Because of their obedience to *occupy* the instruction of their father, they were <u>able</u> to dispossess the inhabitants of their land. They stood in their strength.

The Hearing and Doing Alert

Principle: This grace empowers us to occupy the word of God that has been sown into our hearts—take possession of it.

What: "But be ye doers of the word, and not hearers only,
Why: deceiving your own selves;
For if any be a hearer of the word, and not a doer, he is like unto a man beholding his natural face in a glass: For he beholdeth himself, and goeth his way, and straightway forgetteth what manner of man he was.
How: But whoso looketh into the perfect law of liberty, and continueth therein, he being not a forgetful hearer, but a doer of the work, this man shall be blessed in his deed" (James 1:22-25).

Commentary: Hearers and doers of God's word are not deceived. They remember to occupy: it's what reasonable people do.

Failure to Occupy

In Matthew 7:26, Jesus describes the individual who hears His Word and does not <u>do</u> the Word *that he hears*. He said that he is likened unto a foolish man who built his house upon the sand. The rain descended and the floods came and the winds blew and beat upon that house and it fell and great was the fall of it. One pastor said, "Jesus wanted to make that man rich and famous, but he let his house fall."

That man was a hearer only. He sided with the natural man, not his spirit, and he was deceived. He *neglected* to <u>keep</u> the Word that he had <u>heard</u> in his heart.

To occupy, the Bible says: *he who has shall be given*. In other words, until you do the Word, you don't have the Word. You are self-deceived. So, the foolish are not defeated by the storm, they are defeated by a failure to occupy. Not to occupy becomes a matter of negligence: that being, a failure to perform the reasonable person standard.

4. Grace to Pray

Believing and Receiving

This process of grace guards the *promise*. It focuses on the prayer of faith: believing we receive. It involves our fight against doubt.

I needed to receive a large sum of money. So I prayed and believed that the funds were released into the natural realm, as soon as I had prayed. Doubt, which is the enemy of faith, came immediately to steal the seed that I had sown into my heart. It occurred during my time of devotion. Doubt said: *"What if you don't' get the money?"* I then responded, *"I have already received it."* The doubt left.

However, the next day, the doubt returned saying: *"How will you get it? Who will give it to you?"* My response was the same, *"I have already received it."* After a few days, doubt left, and the money came to me. It was more than enough.

The Deception of Doubt

In Mark 11, Jesus, being hungry, saw a fig tree, afar off, having leaves. Jesus was puzzled since it was not the time of figs. So, as Jesus examined the tree, He saw <u>no figs</u>. He then realized that His conscience was correct; it was not the time of figs. He had been deceived *by doubt* (it made Him question his faith). So, Jesus cursed the fig tree; He did not like being deceived, and it withered up from the roots. Afterwards, He taught His disciples how to attack doubt by praying mountain moving prayers.

In John 1:46, Nathanael, under the influence of doubt, *withheld confidence* toward Nazareth. He responded with *prejudice* when Philip, another disciple, told him that they had found the Lord. Nathanael's response was, "…can any good thing come out of Nazareth?" Philip then challenged him saying, "…come and see." As he complied, doubt was resisted. Jesus then praised Nathanael; for he had no guile.

The Believing and Receiving Alert

The Principle: This grace empowers us to pray effectually. It is a fight to only believe.

What: "…Have faith in God…and shall not doubt in his heart…therefore I say unto you, what things so ever ye desire,
Why: when ye pray,
How: believe that ye receive them, and ye shall have them. And when ye stand praying, forgive…that your Father also which is in heaven may forgive you your trespasses. But if ye do not forgive, neither will your Father which is in heaven forgive your trespasses" (Mark 11:22-26).

Commentary: Prayer is a game changer. It is our only weapon. And when we sin and miss the mark, prayer gives us all one more move. However, so that our prayers are not hindered, we must forgive others, and then our own trespasses *will* also be forgiven!

Failure to Only Believe

In John 11, Lazarus, the brother of Martha and Mary, had taken ill. The sisters sent word to where Jesus was, telling Him that Lazarus was sick. When Jesus heard it, He said that this sickness was not unto death, but for the glory of God. So, Jesus abode two days still in the same place.

When Jesus came, He found that Lazarus had lain in the grave four days already. Someone had stopped <u>believing</u>. Mary said, "Lord, if thou had been here, my brother had not died." Jesus groaned in the spirit and was troubled; then He said, "Where have ye laid him?" In other words, show Me where you stopped believing, and Mary did.

However, prior to seeing Mary, Jesus had edified her sister, Martha, and He had given her a <u>new</u> Word to believe: Your brother shall rise again. Because Martha believed in the resurrection, she could now receive a better promise: a resurrected brother. Then Jesus raised Lazarus.

5. Grace to Dominate

Binding and Loosing

This process of grace guards our *minds*. It focuses on our walk of <u>dominion</u>: binding and loosing; giving us the power to govern and control. It involves binding the bad perceptions and loosing the good.

A few months ago, I had a vision of one of my daughters walking—bent over and weeping. Later, it was revealed that she had recently been dealing with feelings of condemnation: mainly relationship regrets. I told her of my vision, adding that her feelings of guilt, regret, and condemnation were due to false doctrine.

Basically, she was not fighting her thoughts. As a result, her thoughts had left her <u>bound</u>: bent out of shape. After being edified, her perspective changed, and she began to feel better. Her peace of mind had returned.

In Luke 13:10, Jesus was teaching in one of the synagogues on the Sabbath, when He noticed a woman who was bowed together and unable to lift herself up. Jesus said unto her, "Woman, thou are loose from thine infirmity. Then Jesus laid His hands on her and immediately she was made straight and glorified God."

Jesus, in effect, had to change this woman's perspective of herself; He changed her *mindset*. And, the legality of her being a daughter of Abraham caused her to focus on her kingdom rights.

For eighteen years, this woman had heard the voice of her infirmity saying: "You are bound!" Then she heard the voice of the Lord calling her by her redemptive name: *Loosed*. It was refreshing. That truth resonated with her, and it also set her free to walk in her dominion.

And by glorifying God, she strengthened her new identity. She would now see herself from God's point of view.

Without the kingdom of God, we all bow to the image of the <u>fallen nature</u>. This entity, also known as our sin nature, gives us a negative perception of life, ourselves, and of others. If unchecked, it leads us into spiritual bondage: bowing to sin, guilt, regrets, sorrow, and condemnation. It also effectively blinds our minds causing our thoughts to be distorted and our hearts to be troubled. As we bind these distractions, we can then follow peace with all men.

Years ago, I observed a little girl who was struggling while carrying a large, oversized piece of luggage. I said to my colleague, "Look at that little girl trying to carry that large luggage." She responded, "Yes, she is a big help for her mother, isn't she?" Although we both observed the same phenomena, the observation yielded two very different perspectives—one perception driven by the sin nature, the other by grace.

Her point of view effectively loosed my peace, by binding the enemy of my soul.

The Binding and Loosing Alert

The Principle: This grace empowers us to walk in our dominion. It involves the power to restrain the enemy by using *cease and desist* orders to maintain our peace.

What: "Follow peace with all men, and holiness,
Why: without which no man shall see the Lord:
How: Looking diligently lest any man fail of the grace of God; lest any root of bitterness springing up trouble you, and thereby many be defiled" (Hebrews 12:14-15).

Commentary: The enemy searches our hearts for signs of bitterness that have not been forsaken; areas where we have not given grace, but instead, we have become 'accusers of the brethren.' Giving grace to others will maintain the Lordship of Jesus in our lives and peace with all men.

Failure to Bind

In the book of Esther, the story is told of a queen named Vashti—she was King Ahasuerus's first wife before Queen Esther.

The King made a feast and invited all in his province. However, he received a divine influence that his wife, Vashti, had not bound her flesh, but was serving it—she had made her *own separate feast* for the women. She had her own agenda! The king had also heard that she was wearing the *crown royal* and not the royal crown. This was most disturbing.

So, on the seventh day, when the King's heart was merry with wine, he asked his seven chamberlains to bring Vashti, the queen, before him. But queen Vashti refused to come.

Therefore the king's anger burned in him, and he then sought wisdom on how to best handle the situation. He had never given a command that was not heeded.

He was then told that Vashti's behavior not only affected him but other wives would begin to despise their husbands as well. And, that her behavior would gender great contempt throughout his kingdom—adding that every man should bear rule in his own house.

Finally, Vashti was dethroned and the decision was then made to seek a new queen. They found Esther. She required nothing but what was appointed. *Her flesh was bound.* The king loved Esther, and she obtained grace and favour in his sight more than all the other virgins. So he set the *royal crown* upon her head, and he made her queen instead of Vashti.

Then the king made a great feast unto all his princes and his servants, *even* <u>Esther's feast</u>. She did not come with her own agenda; she yielded to grace. Now, the king could bear rule in his own house.

6. Grace to Watch

Watching and Praying

This process of grace guards the *heart*. It focuses on being <u>alert</u>; it involves *troubling the flesh:* our need to fight back!

A couple of years ago, I watched a movie entitled: *Wait Until Dark*. In the movie, Audrey Hepburn played a <u>blind</u> woman who was being conned by three men; each posing as different people. They were looking for an item *hidden in a doll* that was left in her home by a former guest.

Although blind, Audrey paid close attention to the particular nuance of each man, even sensing the pattern of their walk.

She was sober and vigilant. But, because she was unable to locate the item, the antagonist turned to violence. And so did Audrey. First, she decided to even the playing field—she smashed all the lights in the house and made plans to fight back.

The main perpetrator began by first turning against his partners and killing them. They were each caught <u>off guard</u>. Then he went after Audrey. Though blind, she still resisted his every move. She even wounded him. In the end, he died from his wound.

The Holy Spirit said the key to her victory was that she, unlike his partners, <u>fought back</u>! And when we fight, we win.

No Victory without God

My son shared a story where he was warned by his conscience not to engage with a certain group of kids. Ignoring that voice of grace, he did it anyway, and things quickly went south. Reflecting on the incidence, he said, "As I disobeyed (failed to watch), I felt like I was going alone, without God."

When you follow the influence of grace, know that you are not going in alone. And, if things do go south, it becomes a grace battle: where the battle is not yours, but God's.

The Watching and Praying Alert

The Principle: This grace empowers us to detect or prevent, as we maintain a posture of resistance or defense against the wiles of the enemy and the fiery darts of the wicked.

What: "Watch and pray,
Why: that ye enter not into temptation:
How: the spirit indeed is willing, but the flesh is weak" (Matthew 26:41).

Commentary: God wants us to maintain a vigilant watch over our hearts. *Without watching you will pray amiss.* However, as you watch, the flesh is troubled and the spirit wins.

Importunity (troublesome frequency) is the key to troubling the flesh. And, the flesh is overcome by the pain of persistence.

Failure to Watch

In 1 Kings 13, there came a man of God, out of Judah, who had received the divine influence of God upon his heart to cry against the altar in Bethel. He had also received a charge to: eat no bread, not drink water, and not <u>turn</u> again the same way that he came. So he went another way. Being watchful, and vigilant, he <u>stood</u> his ground.

However, there was an old prophet (a type of flesh) who sought him and found him <u>sitting</u> under an oak—not standing his ground. The old prophet then enticed him, saying, "I am a prophet also and an angel spake unto me saying, bring him back with thee into thine house, that he may eat bread and drink water. But he lied to him."

In his simplicity, the man believed the old prophet and went *<u>back</u>* with him, disregarding God's commandment. After his meal, he left and was slain by a lion. Failure to watch the flesh, caused this man of God to turn from his righteousness and be slain. He lacked importunity in his watch.

7. Grace to Sow

Sowing and Reaping

This process of grace guards the *harvest*. It focuses on sowing to the Spirit and not to the flesh. It involves our ability to reap in due season. *Without grace, we will sow to the flesh.*

Not long ago, I had the opportunity to put this process of grace to work. I had spent funds that were outside the allotted budget. I noticed that thoughts were coming to me, questioning how I was going to replace the funds. And without really thinking about it I said, *God will provide it himself.* The negative thoughts continued to come, and I continued to give the same answer.

That next day, my husband, along with our sons, went to pick up our dinner and he found out that his debit card had expired. Before he could respond to the cashier by offering another card, a lady who was waiting for her order, heard what was happening and insisted on paying for our whole meal—a family of five. The amount she paid was equivalent to the amount I had overspent.

When I heard the story, I realized that God had indeed provided. The seed I had spoken promptly possessed the gate of my enemies.

The manifestation of <u>our</u> sown seed is known as 'due season.' By sowing to the Spirt I reaped due season.

God promises that we will all reap in due season, if we do not yield to deception: being weary or fainting. Yielding to the influence of grace (by encouraging myself in the Lord), had placed me in an offensive position, where the ball was in my court. This position allows the supernatural powers of God to have free course to operate in our lives—both in season and out.

Pursue, Overtake, Recover All

In 1 Samuel 30, David and his men returned to their hometown and discovered that the Amalekites had plundered their city. Their wives, their sons, and their daughters, were all taken captive. David and his men wept until they had no more power to weep.

To make matters worse, David's men, being so grieved, spoke of stoning <u>him</u>. But, David *encouraged himself in the Lord.* In seeking wisdom from the Lord, he asked, "Should I pursue after this troop? Shall I overtake them?" God said: "Pursue, for you shall surely overtake them, and without fail recover all."

So David and his men pursued them, and the Bible said David recovered all that the Amalekites had carried away, nothing lacking.

David's men sought the natural way to relieve their pain; they sowed to their flesh. However, David sowed to the Spirit and reaped due season.

The Sowing and Reaping Alert

The Principle: This grace empowers us to reap the harvest, when we do not yield to discouragement.

What: "Be not deceived;
Why: God is not mocked [defeated]: for whatsoever a man soweth, that shall he also reap. For he that soweth to his flesh shall of the flesh reap corruption; but he that soweth to the Spirit shall of the Spirit reap life everlasting.
How: And let us not be weary in well doing: for in due season we shall reap, if we faint not" (Galatians 6:7-9).

Commentary: Both weariness and fainting will mock you. But don't despair, that which you have sown to the Spirit, you will reap in due season. Don't tap out.

Failure to Sow to the Spirit

Matthew 25:14-30, says *the kingdom of heaven* is as a man travelling into a far country, *who* called his own servants, and he delivered unto them his goods. And unto one he gave five talents; to another, two; to another, one. The first two servants turned a profit, received joy, and were able to reign in life. They sowed to the Sprit and reaped in due season.

The last servant did not. He sowed to his flesh and could not reap the harvest that God had laid up for him from the foundation of the world. His talent and its due season were both then taken from him and given to another; he was sentenced to live with the corruption that he had reaped by sowing to his flesh.

By yielding to weariness, he not only missed God, but he missed his due season as well. He failed to encourage himself in the Lord.

Look after each other so that none of you fails to receive the grace of God...

(Hebrews 12:15 (NLT)

Chapter 8

Possessing Your Possessions

In 1 Samuel 17, David's Father, Jesse, certainly heard from God when he sent David to *look after the welfare of his three older brothers:* soldiers in King Saul's army. David's father sent him, the youngest; even though there were four, older sons, still at home. The decision to send David was the influence of grace on the father's heart; grace thinks outside the box.

When David arrived on the scene, he found the two armies facing off as would be expected, but there was an additional threat: a Philistine giant named Goliath.

Because of Goliath, this was not an ordinary battle; for this was not an attack against their natural abilities; that is, their willingness to perform the familiar. Instead, Goliath was challenging their <u>capabilities</u>. It was an attack against their *access* to grace; their ability to do something that had never been done before. That made the attack supernatural.

The Bible says Goliath (a type of flesh) had been there forty days and forty nights defying Israel. The Philistine said, "I defy the armies of Israel this day." According to the Bible, when Saul and all Israel heard those words of the Philistine, they were dismayed and greatly afraid. *Now, this was a case against grace:*
Their Case: Dismay, fear.
Their Breach: Perverseness (being worried and wearisome) had made the armies of Israel cosmic criminals. Now this case must be litigated by scripture; failure to triumph.

Goliath knew that to defy Israel, he would have to get them to worry; then God would find perverseness in them and they could then be defeated. This would be done by getting them to speak *his* words. The plan almost worked; however, God had one more move, and his name was David.

The men of Israel then informed David of the threat from the giant. They said it was to *defy Israel*. They were already speaking Goliath's words. David identified the problem right away. The men of Israel had failed to discern truth from falsehood. They were *not* echoing the influence of grace; they were voicing the words of the enemy, saying: "Surely to defy Israel is he come up." As they sowed those words into their hearts, they began to be weary and a breach was created. David knew then that he was there to repair that breach.

David then inquired of the rewards that the victor should receive for killing Goliath. He was told: "… the king will enrich him with great riches, and will give him his daughter, and make his father's house free in Israel."

After hearing the spoils that were involved, David took the case.

However, David's oldest brother became offended, criticized him, accused him of pride, and also questioned his motives.

David had not received any influence from God to fight with his brother. So, he knew that this was an attempt to defy him—to get him enraged: to get him out of the spirit and into his flesh. But, David had learned to pick his battles—fight only causes ordained by God. After all, he was there to check on their welfare, so that none failed to receive the grace of God.

But before he could prevail over Goliath, David had to first prove that he could pass the *perverseness* test: the ability to keep a wholesome tongue, even while being *accused by his brother*. He had to show dominion over his own emotions. David stayed the course, and responded in grace. He answered his brother and said,

"...Is there not a cause [a case]?" David then turned away from him and focused on the *case* at hand. David realized that cases, once they are challenged, would afford him the opportunity to *possess his possessions.*

So David began working the seven processes of grace:

- ✓ According to the divine influence of God upon his heart, he *discerned* that the attack was to defy the armies of the *living God,* not Israel. The men of Israel had left God out of the equation.
- ✓ David then bought the field: to *overcome,* he counted it all joy. He knew that joy would overcome worry. So, he ran to the battle.
- ✓ To David, this fight against Goliath was his reasonable service: one that any prudent man would *occupy:* as he said, "Is there not a cause?"

Not to fight this type of battle would be negligent. He had to fight worry.

✓ Afterwards, he made his *prayer* of confession: "The Lord will deliver me from the hand of this Philistine."

✓ He then took *dominion*: he refused the king's armor; he would use God's armor.

✓ As he *watched* his heart: he received and obeyed a contrary instruction: take five smooth stones. The number five to reference the number of grace. God was yelling: Use grace!

✓ Then David *sowed* to the Spirit: He only spoke words of faith, while being mocked by Goliath.

As David followed the processes of grace, he was triumphant over the giant: *those things (inhabitants) that man-handle us;* and he received the promised spoils.

In fighting battles that challenge our capabilities, grace is sufficient to empower us to possess our possessions.

The Perverseness Alert

This alert calls for us not to be tempted to act in opposition to what is proper.

What: "Behold, I have received commandment to bless: and he hath blessed; and I cannot reverse it.
Why: He hath not beheld iniquity in Jacob, neither hath he seen *perverseness* in Israel:
How: the LORD his God *is* with him, and the shout of a king *is* among them"

(Numbers 23:20-21).

The shout of a king is the shout of joy, <u>triumph,</u> and exultation. Giants of worry are put to flight as we keep our joy. And, joy is non-reversible.

But upon mount Zion shall be deliverance, and there shall be holiness; and the house of Jacob shall possess their possessions.

(Obadiah 1:17)

Conclusion

Receiving a Contrary Instruction

My sister shares the story of an incident that left her in awe of the grace of God. As a single mom, working on commission, she found herself going from feast to famine as her income fluctuated. Consequently, over time, frequent threats, moves, and evictions were commonplace. Although she had an affinity for high income residences, evictions plagued her in low income ones, as well. Moving had just become the norm for her. Out of thirteen total moves, many were plagued by evictions. It had become a vicious cycle. Her breach: peace in a negative situation.

Finally, her peace was challenged; then she sought to break the curse, vowing never to have another eviction notice.

Shortly after making this vow, she perceived that God was prompting her to move again. This instruction was contrary to her natural mind and not self-serving; so she made the move. Then, in that new location, she struggled from time to time, but the funds continued to flow. She then maintained the same residence for four years, without incident. She had set a record, and the curse had been broken.

Recently; however, she received a new threat of eviction. She pled her case to God, praying: *You placed me here, you told me to move and now I'm being threatened with another eviction!*

God then gave her a new strategy: *Stay the course and keep your faith.* The owner grievously provoked her with his demands, and he refused all of her attempts to reconcile. Instead, he gave her a short deadline to move. Although incensed, she still kept her eyes on God, who encouraged her to keep her peace: saying, "This is not your fight." In other words, by receiving the influence of grace, this fight became God's battle, not hers. It was a grace battle.

After maintaining her peace, she noticed that the owner had changed his tune. He asked her how much time she would need to move. Within herself, she figured an additional three months. To her surprise, he renewed her lease. Glory to God!

But she wasn't out of the woods yet. She had to come up with the current rent to consummate the new lease, and the deadline was one week away.

That week she did <u>earn</u> enough money to make the payment, but her current contractor began making it difficult for her to pick up her check; he even attempted to lower the amount owed. But time after time she stood her ground. She was relentless. She demanded every cent.

Eventually, she received all that was due her and she paid her obligation. The eviction was officially stayed.

In hindsight, we see that both the money to consummate the lease and the extended lease itself had been laid up for her, to offset yet another eviction. But without grace, she could not have received it. The curse would have continued.

By receiving grace, she was able to flow in her anointing: that God given ability that empowers us to operate in concert with our spirit—the place of maturity. Her spirit then positioned her to receive her kingdom inheritance.

For starters, she would have to know how to be abased and how to abound (when to fight and when to forbear); with the contractor: *stand your ground*; with the landlord: *forbear*. As grace flowed, the wisdom of God flowed. And she received her turnaround.

And it all began by receiving an instruction *contrary* to the thinking of her natural mind—we call it: Grace.

Epilogue

A few months ago, I was dismayed dealing with a family issue that frankly, disturbed my peace. As I looked to the Holy Spirit, He spoke to me and said, "I gave you five." I knew that He was referring to the parable of the talents. I thought, *really!* I remembered that those with five talents turned them into ten and were rewarded. If I already have five that would mean that I have been previously equipped and pre-qualified to be victorious over situations that I might encounter. That perspective changed my view on handling difficult situations. Now, all God has to say to me when I am facing a challenge is, "I gave you five," and the rest is gospel.

As you know, your spirit—the real you—is inditing a good matter. It is there that we are partakers of God's divine nature. He has given to us gifts, talents, skills, and abilities. In the parable of the talents, it is there, in our inner man, that God has graced us with five talents. This grace has pre-qualified us to deal with the tests, trials, and circumstances of life. Regardless of the challenges we are facing, *the die has been cast*; we are already equipped, and we are well prepared for the task. Now, the Helper is waiting on each of us to say, "Lord, you gave me five, and I have gained five more."

The Holy Spirit is our Helper. He delights in giving us divine aid to assist us in knowing God's will and to enlighten us. Here, He prompts us to ask the Father.

So, as we personalize the seven processes of grace, the Helper will empower us to walk by what we believe; not by what we see. The key lies in our commitment: to **fight back** (confess our faith); to receive an **instruction contrary** to our own thoughts (follow the leading of our spirit); and to **stand** (in our place of authority). Then we will possess our possessions, that is, we will possess our thoughts of faith.

94

The Grace Roadmap

Grace to Discern: *Guards our Will*

Grace to   Overcome: *Guards our Joy*

Grace to Occupy: *Guards the Word*

Grace to Pray: *Guards our Faith*

Grace to Dominate: *Guards our Minds*

Grace to Watch: *Guards our Hearts*

Grace to Sow: *Guards the Harvest*

That if thou shalt confess with thy mouth the Lord Jesus, and shalt believe in thine heart that God hath raised him from the dead, thou shalt be saved. For with the heart man believeth unto righteousness; and with the mouth confession is made unto salvation.

(Romans 10:9-10)

Salvation Prayer

Father, I believe that Jesus is the Son of God. And that He was raised from the dead for my justification. Jesus, come into my heart and take over my life; be my Lord and Savior. Your Word says: Ask and you shall receive. For everyone who asks, receives. I believe I receive You now in Jesus' Name, Amen.

For we walk by faith, not by sight:

(2 Corinthians 5:7)

*Walk by what you believe,
not by what you see.*

About the Author

Carolyn Chambers is a licensed minister and a member of Faith Ministerial Alliance. She is a celebrated Christian author, and is best known for her groundbreaking work: *Discovering Your Anointing Numbers: Allow me to introduce you to Yourself.*

She and her husband, Keith, have also developed Anointing Profiles that yield personalized commentaries based on birth demographics.

Carolyn holds a Bachelor's degree from the University of Wisconsin and a Master's degree from the University of Arizona. She and her husband live in Phoenix, Arizona, with their two sons: Nehemiah and Zacharias. They are members of Pilgrim Rest Baptist Church.

Other Books by Carolyn Chambers

DISCOVERING YOUR ANOINTING NUMBERS

**Carolyn
Chambers**

In her life-changing
new book, Carolyn
Chambers helps
readers discover their
anointing numbers
and empower them to fight life's great
battle-themselves. Simply put—everyone is
at war with *self*. But walking anointed is
something everyone can achieve.

In, "Discovering Your Anointing Numbers:
Allow me to introduce you to Yourself,"
Carolyn Chambers examines the influence
that birth demographics have on human
behavior. This is a compelling read for all.

THE ANOINTED LIFE- *Crucifying the Flesh*

Carolyn Chambers

The Anointed Life: **Powerful New Book by Celebrated Christian Author Proves Flesh is the True "Enemy of the Soul"**

Everyone faces adversity and tests in life but some pass where others fail. While faith and the word of God explain why these patterns exist, millions still search for answers. In her compelling new book, the author exposes the true enemy of the soul – the flesh. "Simply put," she says, "everybody is at war with themselves."

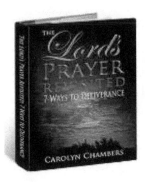

THE LORD'S PRAYER -- REVISITED

7 WAYS TO DELIVERENCE

Carolyn Chambers

Praying the Lord's Prayer is the Answer
 Understanding The Lord's Prayer is the Solution!

Understanding is the key to whether we have solutions in life or just answers. The Lord's Prayer – Revisited gives us the understanding we need to examine the enemy's front line of offense: self—and its undercover role in the attacks against our lives. The Lord's Prayer disrupts the plans of the wicked and scatters the enemy of our soul *seven* ways.

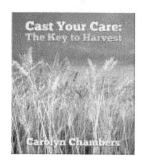

Cast Your Care:

The Key to Harvest

Carolyn Chambers

Care Keeps the Attack There!

Heaven is looking for joy. Without joy, we have no strength; without strength there is no presence of God, and our prayers are hindered. The flesh, our animal nature, uses care to attack our joy.

Moreover, when we are in the flesh, we can't bear up under pressure. But, unlike animals, we have a choice. We can choose to cast our care; and when we do, we are in the spirit, then all of heaven will work on our behalf; and our prayers are unhindered.